Mind Benders

Mind Benders

100 Logic Games and Puzzles to Improve Your
Memory, Exercise Your Brain, and Keep Your Mind Sharp

DAVID MILLAR

Skyhorse Publishing

Skyhorse Publishing books may be purchased in bulk at special discounts for sales promotion, corporate gifts, fund-raising, or educational purposes. Special editions can also be created to specifications. For details, contact the Special Sales Department, Skyhorse Publishing, 307 West 36th Street, 11th Floor, New York, NY 10018 or info@skyhorsepublishing.com.

Skyhorse® and Skyhorse Publishing® are registered trademarks of Skyhorse Publishing, Inc.®, a Delaware corporation.

Visit our website at www.skyhorsepublishing.com.

10 9 8 7 6 5 4 3

Library of Congress Cataloging-in-Publication Data is available on file.

Cover design by Brian Peterson

Print ISBN: 978-1-5107-3542-2

Printed in the United States of America

Contents

Puzzles

Symbol Sums 1

The sums of five combinations of symbols have been provided. What is the value of each individual symbol?

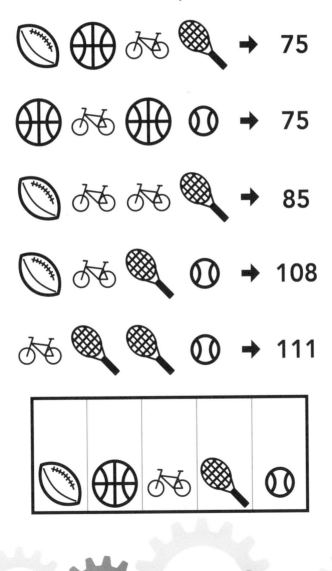

Cube Logic 1

Which of the four foldable patterns can be folded
to make the cube displayed?

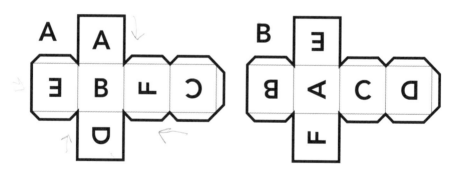

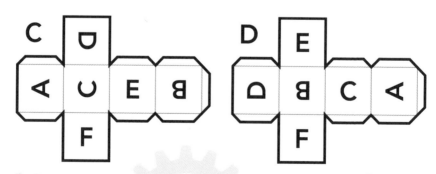

Tetra Grid 1

Drop each of the shapes into the grid in the order provided to spell ten six-letter words. Clues for the words have been provided next to the grid.

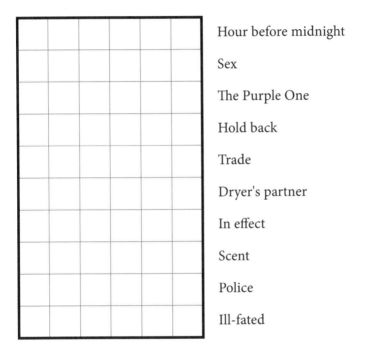

Hour before midnight

Sex

The Purple One

Hold back

Trade

Dryer's partner

In effect

Scent

Police

Ill-fated

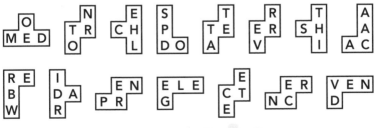

Story Logic 1

A local hotel is hosting an internet convention for the first time, and things are getting a bit wild. Use the clues to help convention staff return some lost items to the right people in the right rooms.

		Room Number					Lost Item					Fandom				
		Room 811	Room 812	Room 813	Room 814	Room 815	Cowboy Hat	Lanyard	Plastic Sword	Pocketwatch	Utility Belt	Anime	Card Games	Role Playing	Science Fiction	Vlogging
Attendee	Kirsten															
	Leigh															
	Molly															
	Nupur															
	Oliver															
Fandom	Anime															
	Card Games															
	Role Playing															
	Science Fiction															
	Vlogging															
Lost Item	Cowboy Hat															
	Lanyard															
	Plastic Sword															
	Pocketwatch															
	Utility Belt															

The card game enthusiast stays directly across from the owner of the pocketwatch.

Oliver, the role player, stays in the room directly across from the lanyard's owner.

Molly's room is on the same side of the hall as vending, and is directly across from Oliver's room.

Leigh and the attendee who lost their plastic sword have rooms on the same side of the hallway.

The attendee missing their plastic sword is not into role playing games.

The attendee that stays in the room directly next to the elevator is a vlogger.

The cowboy hat belongs to either Kristen or Oliver.

Either Kirsten or Molly is a science fiction enthusiast.

Nupur's room is directly adjacent to either the stairs or the vending machines.

The anime lover is the owner of either the utility belt or the cowboy hat.

Vending	814	815	Elevators	801
Stairs	813	812	811	810

Maze 1

Find your way from the top to the bottom.

Word Sudoku 1

In the sudoku grid, enter one of each of six unique letters into each row, column, and rectangle without repetition.

SKI RUN

Triangulate 1–5

Use one letter from each triangle, in order from
left to right, to make three related words. Each
letter will be used once.

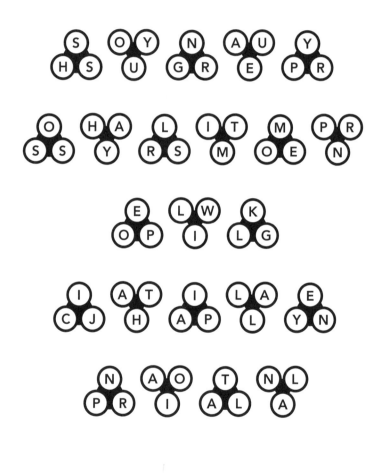

Numcross 1

Use the provided clues to fill the grid with numbers. No entry may start with a 0.

A	B	C		D	E
F				G	
		H	I		
J	K				
L			M	N	O
P			Q		

Across		Down	
A.	A down × D across	A.	B down - 9
D.	Square root of E down	B.	Half of O down
F.	G across + O down	C.	Consecutive digits in
G.	2 × A down		ascending order
H.	J across + 1600	D.	A perfect square
J.	I down + 400	E.	Another perfect square
L.	4 × A down	I.	H across - 2000
M.	Consecutive digits in	J.	One-third of K down
	ascending order	K.	Consecutive digits in
P.	D across + 2		descending order
Q.	2 × O down	N.	P across × 4
		O.	J down - E down

Rearrangement 1–2

Rearrange the letters in the phrase "HERBED MANIAC" to spell something an enthusiastic foodie might keep in their kitchen.

Rearrange the letters in the phrase "INK DOT GOOBERS" to spell something the author used when writing this book.

Symbol Sums 2

The sums of five combinations of symbols have been provided. What is the value of each individual symbol?

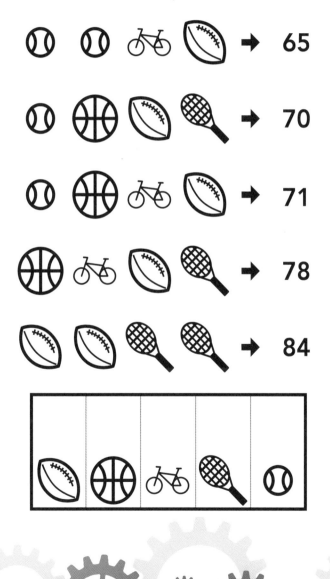

Tetra Grid 2

Drop each of the shapes into the grid in the order provided to spell ten six-letter words. Clues for the words have been provided next to the grid.

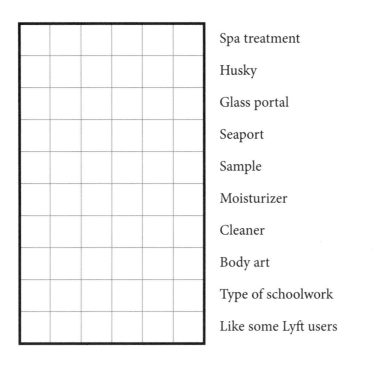

Spa treatment

Husky

Glass portal

Seaport

Sample

Moisturizer

Cleaner

Body art

Type of schoolwork

Like some Lyft users

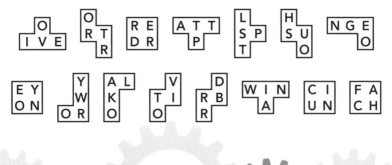

Arrow Maze 1

Each move, jump from your current square to another square in the same row, column, or diagonal as permitted by the arrow provided. There are no dead ends here. Can you get from Start to Finish in 9 steps?

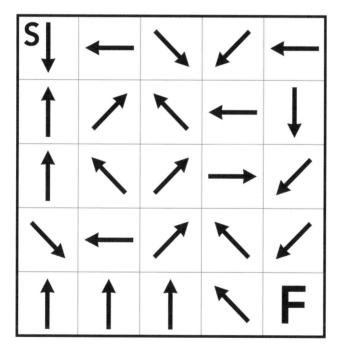

Hashtags 1

Use the hashtag clues provided to fill the grid with eight words. Four words with three letters should span the white squares in each row and column, skipping shaded squares. Four words with five letters use the full rows and columns.

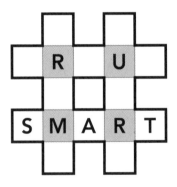

Threes

#Crusty #Dessert

#Shout

#Party

#Seated

Fives

#Amazon #FreeShipping

#Brainy

#Crew

#TikkaMasala

Two words have been completed to get you started!

Big Sandwich 1–2

Stuff the space between the slices of bread, one letter per polygon, so that two words read down each column and two words read across the filling of the sandwich. The filling will form a phrase or compound word.

RI	LE	BE	S	MA
		E		
		N		
E	D	T	INT	H

Across Clue: Clothing

RO	ME	BO	WA	BEL
E	T	S	T	S

Across Clue: Gardening

Two words have been completed to get you started!

Word Sudoku 2

In the sudoku grid, enter one of each of six unique letters into each row, column, and rectangle without repetition.

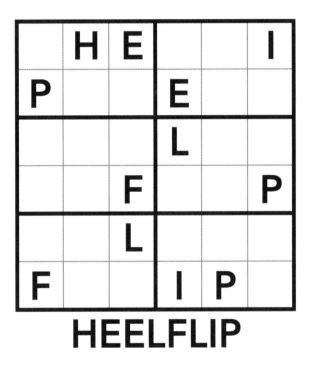

HEELFLIP

Triangulate 6–10

Use one letter from each triangle, in order from left to right, to make three related words. Each letter will be used once.

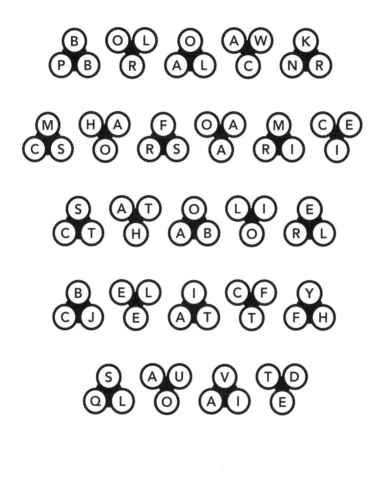

Story Logic 2

To facilitate a new high-speed rail line, four train bridges with very low clearance are slated to be replaced in the coming year. Use the clues to match the bridge to its original clearance, cost of replacement, and project start date.

		Cost				Project Start				Original Height			
		$1.1 Million	$1.6 Million	$2.1 Million	$2.6 Million	January	April	July	October	10' 5"	11' 8"	11' 10"	12' 1"
Cross Street	Parker St.												
	Quincy Blvd.												
	Roosevelt Dr.												
	Seventh Ave.												
Original Height	10' 5"												
	11' 8"												
	11' 10"												
	12' 1"												
Project Start	January												
	April												
	July												
	October												

The original Parker St. bridge has a higher clearance than the most expensive project's original bridge.

The 11' 8" bridge project will begin before the bridge on Seventh Ave. bridge project.

The Quincy Blvd. bridge project will begin before the replacement of the bridge with the lowest clearance.

The project with the January start date is the cheapest.

The project starting in April is replacing a bridge whose current clearance is higher than the Parker St. bridge.

The bridge with a clearance of 12' 1" is not projected to be the most or the least expensive to replace.

The project in July has a cost estimate $1 million more than the April project.

The Seventh Ave. bridge is planned to cost less than the replacement of the bridge whose clearance is 11' 10".

The Roosevelt Dr. bridge project will begin in July.

The 11' 10" bridge project has an estimated cost of $2.1 million.

Numcross 2

Use the provided clues to fill the grid with numbers. No entry may start with a 0.

A	B		C	D	E
F			G		
H		I			
		J		K	L
M	N			O	
P				Q	

Across

A. A perfect square
C. 5 × D down
F. N down - E down
G. 7 × E down
H. C down - G across
J. C down × 5
M. Another perfect square
O. Another perfect square
P. Consecutive digits in ascending order
Q. A prime number

Down

A. (A across × 10) + 1
B. Two-fifths of G across
C. (B down × 10) - 1
D. Another perfect square
E. 2 × D down
I. K down × 5
K. A palindrome
L. Consecutive digits in ascending order
M. Square root of M across
N. Another perfect square

Maze 2

Find your way from the top to the bottom.

Arrow Maze 2

Each move, jump from your current square to another square in the same row, column, or diagonal as permitted by the arrow provided. There are no dead ends here. Can you get from Start to Finish in 12 steps?

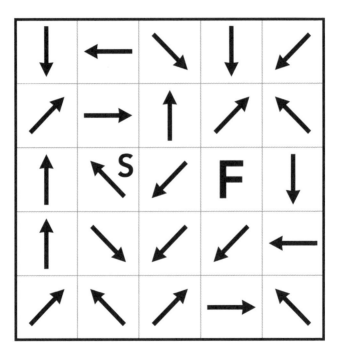

Hashtags 2

Use the hashtag clues provided to fill the grid with eight words. Four words with three letters should span the white squares in each row and column, skipping shaded squares. Four words with five letters use the full rows and columns.

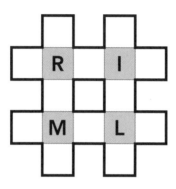

Threes

#GettingSomeSun

#OnTheDL

#Primate

#PutALidOnIt

Fives

#Goofy

#LegPain

#Lots

#Railroad #Amtrak

Cube Logic 2

Which of the four foldable patterns can be folded
to make the cube displayed?

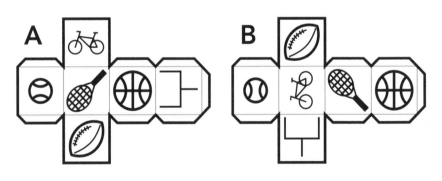

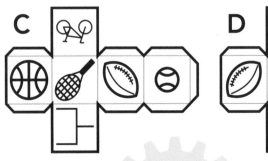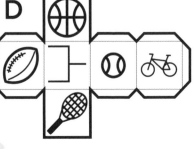

Symbol Sums 3

The sums of five combinations of symbols have been provided. What is the value of each individual symbol?

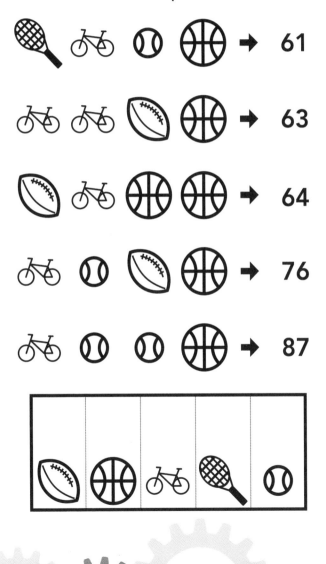

Rearrangement 3–4

Rearrange the letters in the phrase "ELF OWNS CAFE" to spell something one might find at an ice cream parlor.

Rearrange the letters in the phrase "CLIENT ASLEEP" to spell something you might fall asleep waiting to obtain.

Word Sudoku 3

In the sudoku grid, enter one of each of six unique letters into each row, column, and rectangle without repetition.

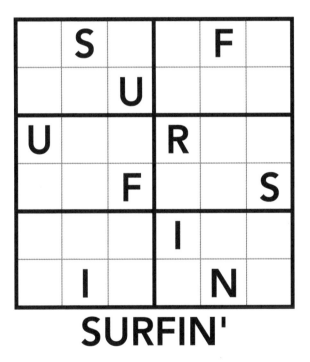

SURFIN'

Story Logic 3

Local farms are working with a co-op to create a meal-prep kit delivered daily to customers. Use the clues about this week's deliveries to match the day of the week to the farm, dish, and average star rating for the dish.

		Weekday				Star Rating				Farm			
		Monday	Tuesday	Wednesday	Thursday	2 Stars	3.5 Stars	4.5 Stars	5 Stars	Johnson Farms	Kale River Farms	Lincoln Ranch	Midas Dairy & Co.
Dish	Eggplant Tart												
	Fresh Tomato Pasta												
	Pepper Steak												
	Stir-Fried Squash												
Farm	Johnson Farms												
	Kale River Farms												
	Lincoln Ranch												
	Midas Dairy & Co.												
Star Rating	2 Stars												
	3.5 Stars												
	4.5 Stars												
	5 Stars												

The highest-rated meal kit was from the day after the meal kit featuring fresh tomato pasta.

The dish using ingredients from Kale River Farms was neither the best dish nor the worst dish of the week according to user ratings.

The stir-fried squash was rated higher than Thursday's meal kit, but not as high as the kit featuring the pepper steak main dish.

Wednesday's meal, which was not the stir-fried squash, used ingredients sourced from Johnson Farms.

The Tuesday meal kit was rated higher than the kit featuring eggplant tart, but lower than the meal kit using ingredients sourced from Midas Dairy & Co.

Triangulate 11–15

Use one letter from each triangle, in order from left to right, to make three related words. Each letter will be used once.

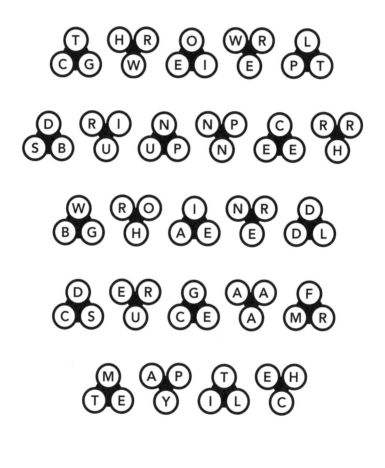

Numcross 3

Use the provided clues to fill the grid with numbers. No entry may start with a 0.

		A	B	C	
	D				
E		■	F		G
H		I	■	J	
	K		L		
	M				

Across

A. Consecutive digits in descending order
D. A palindrome
E. J across × 2
F. I down - 100
H. 2 × E across
J. A perfect cube
K. I down × 10
M. H across × 2

Down

A. A perfect square
B. M across + E down
C. K across × 2
D. Contains one of each even digit: 0, 2, 4, 6, 8
E. E across - 3
G. J across - 10
I. 3 × B down
L. Another perfect square

Tetra Grid 3

Drop each of the shapes into the grid in the order provided to spell ten six-letter words. Clues for the words have been provided next to the grid.

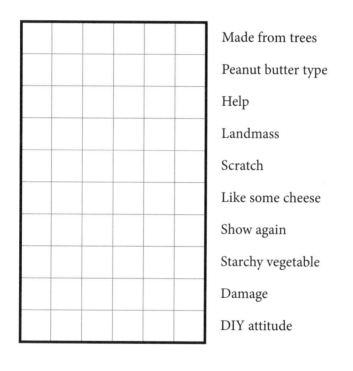

Made from trees

Peanut butter type

Help

Landmass

Scratch

Like some cheese

Show again

Starchy vegetable

Damage

DIY attitude

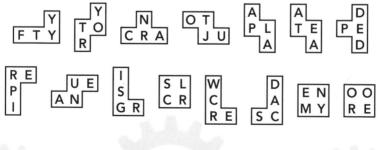

Symbol Sums 4

The sums of five combinations of symbols have been provided. What is the value of each individual symbol?

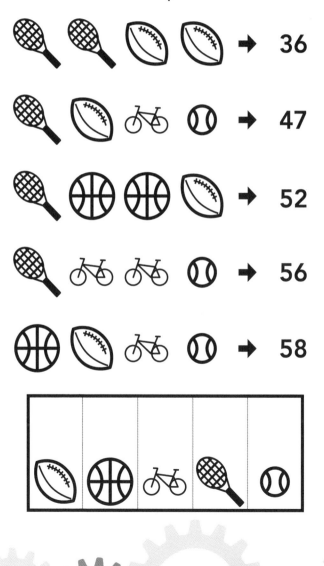

Hashtags 3

Use the hashtag clues provided to fill the grid with eight words. Four words with three letters should span the white squares in each row and column, skipping shaded squares. Four words with five letters use the full rows and columns.

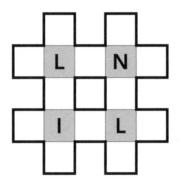

Threes

#Cushion

#Era

#Large

#MoneyMakers

Fives

#Jewelry

#Meadow

#Plot

#Tartan

Cube Logic 3

Which of the four foldable patterns can be folded
to make the cube displayed?

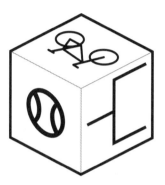

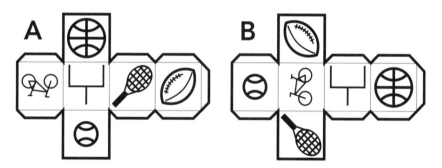

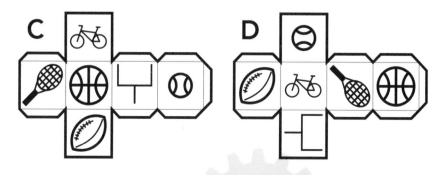

Numcross 4

Use the provided clues to fill the grid with numbers. No entry may start with a 0.

A	B	C		D	E
F				G	
		H	I		
J	K				
L			M	N	O
P			Q		

Across

A. (L across × 11) + 1
D. A perfect square
F. J down - 15
G. Another perfect square
H. Digits that sum to 17
J. D down × 4
L. G across - 1
M. Another perfect square
P. Square root of M across
Q. 5 × O down

Down

A. A number in the Fibonacci sequence
B. N down + O down
C. Consecutive digits in ascending order
D. J down + 300
E. F across × 9
I. Consecutive digits in descending order
J. Another perfect square
K. 2 × M across
N. P across + 2
O. 2 × N down

Triangulate 16–20

Use one letter from each triangle, in order from left to right, to make three related words. Each letter will be used once.

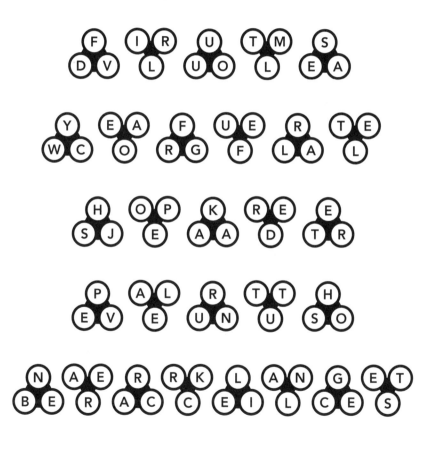

Word Sudoku 4

In the sudoku grid, enter one of each of six unique letters into each row, column, and rectangle without repetition.

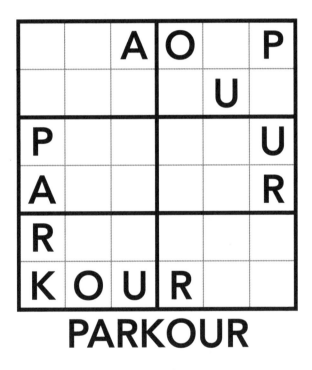

PARKOUR

Symbol Sums 5

The sums of five combinations of symbols have been provided. What is the value of each individual symbol?

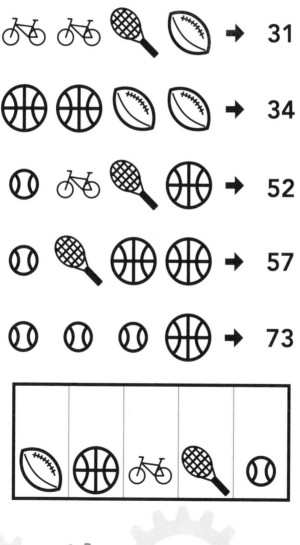

Big Sandwich 3–4

Stuff the space between the slices of bread, one letter per polygon, so that two words read down each column and two words read across the filling of the sandwich.

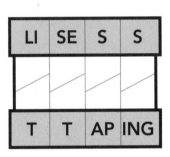

LI	SE	S	S
T	T	AP	ING

Across Clue: Weather

OR	CH	S	S	L	T
S	MP	AR	ATE	E	AM

Across Clue: Dessert

Tetra Grid 4

Drop each of the shapes into the grid in the order provided to spell ten six-letter words. Clues for the words have been provided next to the grid.

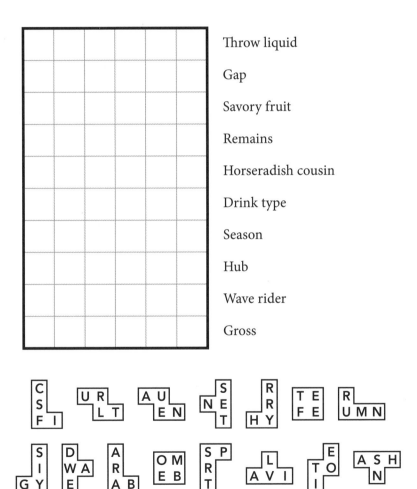

Throw liquid

Gap

Savory fruit

Remains

Horseradish cousin

Drink type

Season

Hub

Wave rider

Gross

Triangulate 21–25

Use one letter from each triangle, in order from left to right, to make three related words. Each letter will be used once.

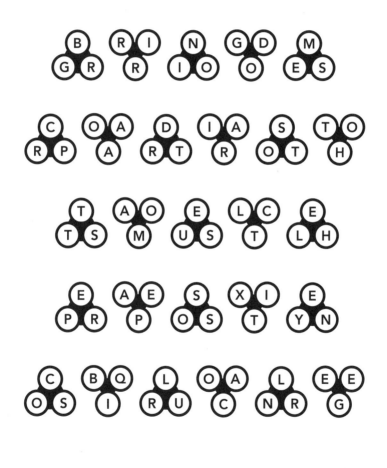

Rearrangement 5–6

Rearrange the letters in the phrase "NEW CONDO FEE" to spell something one shares with their neighbor.

Rearrange the letters in the phrase "RED ALPHA CROP" to spell an agricultural location.

Numcross 5

Use the provided clues to fill the grid with numbers. No entry may start with a 0.

A	B			C	D
E			F		
G		H			
		I		J	K
L	M			N	
O				P	

Across

A. Days in February in a leap year
C. Square root of L across
E. Days in October in a leap year
F. Total days in a leap year
G. H down × 5
I. G across - J down
L. A perfect square
N. L down + P across
O. 2 × L down
P. Another perfect square

Down

A. Consecutive digits in ascending order
B. L across, scrambled
C. Another perfect square
D. Another perfect square
F. F across - 10
H. A palindrome
J. B down + P across + 1
K. (2 × F across) - 1
L. C across - 1
M. A perfect cube

Arrow Maze 3

Each move, jump from your current square to another square in the same row, column, or diagonal as permitted by the arrow or arrows provided. There are no dead ends here. Can you get from Start to Finish in 9 steps?

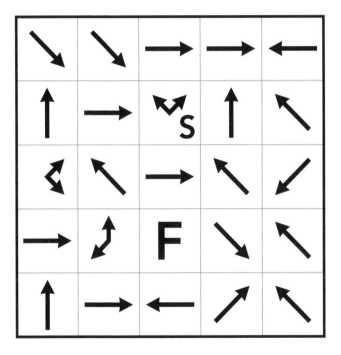

Symbol Sums 6

The sums of five combinations of symbols have been provided. What is the value of each individual symbol?

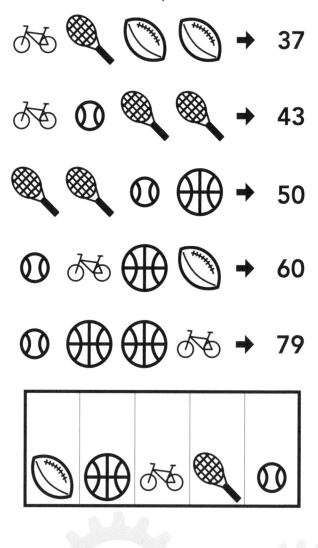

Hashtags 4

Use the hashtag clues provided to fill the grid with eight words. Four words with three letters should span the white squares in each row and column, skipping shaded squares. Four words with five letters use the full rows and columns.

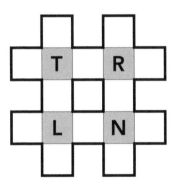

Threes

#Belly

#Dialup

#Sauce #Tofu #Bean

#WheelOfFortune

Fives

#Bikini #Islands

#Factory

#Recruit

#Tale

Story Logic 4

The coffee shop has a number of regulars who come in at the same time every day and order their usual. Use the clues to piece together the daily routine.

		Approximate Time					Drink Order				
		7:30 AM	8:30 AM	10:45 AM	11:45 AM	12:45 PM	Dirty Chai	Espresso Con Panna	Green Tea	Maple Latte	White Mocha
Regular	Becky										
	Chandra										
	Dante										
	Eduardo										
	Fabian										
Drink Order	Dirty Chai										
	Espresso Con Panna										
	Green Tea										
	Maple Latte										
	White Mocha										

Becky usually comes in an hour after Eduardo, who orders a dirty chai (chai latte with an espresso shot).

The regulars who get a white mocha and a maple latte come in back to back.

The regular who orders an espresso con panna comes in an hour before Dante.

Fabian comes in for his drink between the regulars who get a green tea and white mocha, in some order.

The regular who gets a maple latte comes in later than any other regular.

PE Class 1

Use the clues provided to find five answers
starting with the letters PE.

P E _ _ _   Basil, pine nuts, cheese

P E _ _ _   Bird hangout spot

P E _ _ _   Lincoln's home

P E _ _ _   Mario's princess

P E _ _ _ _ _   Waiting for verification

Cube Logic 4

Which of the four foldable patterns can be folded
to make the cube displayed?

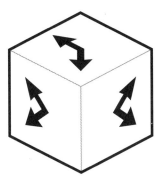

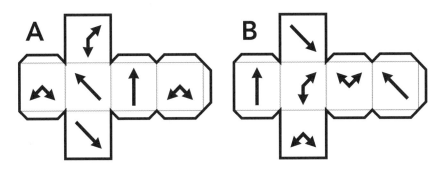

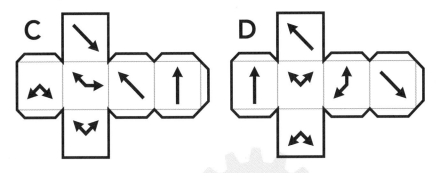

Maze 3

Find your way from the top to the bottom.

Tetra Grid 5

Drop each of the shapes into the grid in the order provided to spell ten six-letter words. Clues for the words have been provided next to the grid.

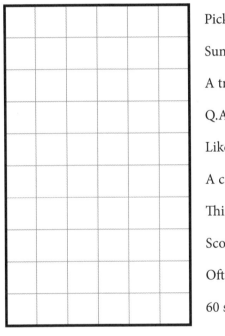

Pickled cabbage dish

Sundae topper

A traffic-light color

Q.A. role

Like some luggage

A continent

Third place

Scottish drink

Oft-spicy vegetable

60 seconds

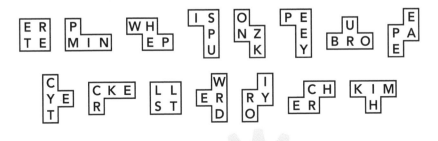

Numcross 6

Use the provided clues to fill the grid with numbers. No entry may start with a 0.

	A	B		
C			D	E
F		■	G	
H	■	I		
J	K			■
■	L		■	

Across

A. B down + 1
C. Contains one of each even digit: 0, 2, 4, 6, 8
F. I down + 1
G. A multiple of B down
H. The answer to life, the universe, & everything
I. Consecutive digits in ascending order
J. C down × 10
L. A US coin value in ¢

Down

A. A across squared
B. A US coin value in ¢
C. Digits that sum to 22
D. 8 × E down
E. A down × 5
F. I across + 3
I. A skateboard move
K. A US coin value in ¢

Big Sandwich 5–6

Stuff the space between the slices of bread, one letter per polygon, so that two words read down each column and two words read across the filling of the sandwich. The filling will form a phrase or compound word.

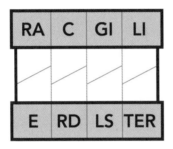

RA	C	GI	LI
E	RD	LS	TER

Across Clue: 18 Holes

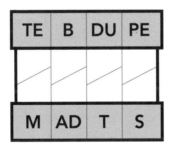

TE	B	DU	PE
M	AD	T	S

Across Clue: Highway

Rearrangement 7–8

Rearrange the letters in the phrase "A CALM CORNER" to spell a sweet treat folks will enjoy.

Rearrange the letters in the phrase "METAL FREAK" to spell a place where you might find a lot of secondhand metal amongst other wares.

Tetra Grid 6

Drop each of the shapes into the grid in the order provided to spell ten six-letter words. Clues for the words have been provided next to the grid.

Measuring system

Baby garment

A continent

Type of fish

1996 horror movie

Vinyl

Dessicate

Forum topic

Beat

Ice cream dish

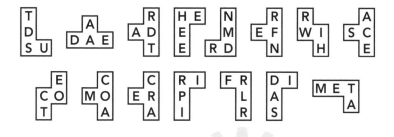

Hashtags 5

Use the hashtag clues provided to fill the grid with eight words. Four words with three letters should span the white squares in each row and column, skipping shaded squares. Four words with five letters use the full rows and columns.

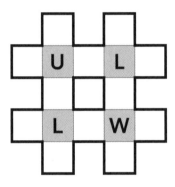

Threes

#Auction

#Doomtree #Rapper

#Prisoner

#Shriek

Fives

#Stooge

#Construct

#Goof #Bozo

#SnowDay #Trucks

Symbol Sums 7

The sums of five combinations of symbols have been provided. What is the value of each individual symbol?

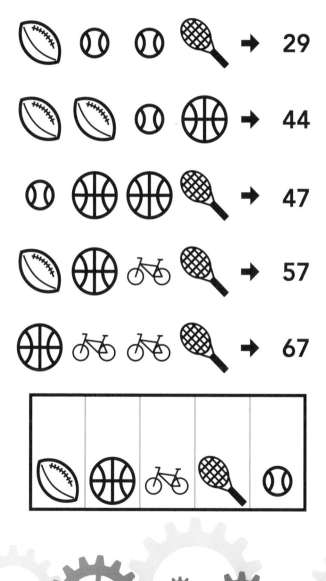

Story Logic 5

It's busy working in Human Resources, and today there are five candidates interviewing for jobs. Use the clues to match the interviewer with the time of the interview and the department hiring.

		Interview Time					Department				
		9:30 AM	10:30 AM	11:30 AM	2:30 PM	3:30 PM	Human Resources	IT/Development	Marketing	Research	Sales
Candidate	Donna										
	Esther										
	Filipe										
	Gozde										
	Harold										
Department	Human Resources										
	IT/Development										
	Marketing										
	Research										
	Sales										

The Marketing department interview takes place in the afternoon.

Esther's interview is scheduled for 11:30 AM.

Donna, who is interviewing for Human Resources, is scheduled to interview in the time slot after the time slot where the Sales Team is holding its interview.

Felipe is either interviewing for the Sales Team or the Research department.

The interview for the IT and Development department is after Harold's interview, but before Gozde's interview.

The Research department interview is in the time slot immediately before the Marketing department.

Cube Logic 5

Which of the four foldable patterns can be folded
to make the cube displayed?

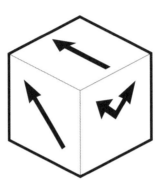

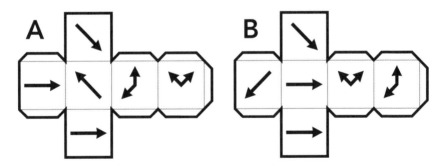

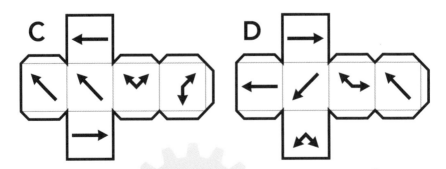

Word Sudoku 5

In the sudoku grid, enter one of each of six unique letters into each row, column, and rectangle without repetition.

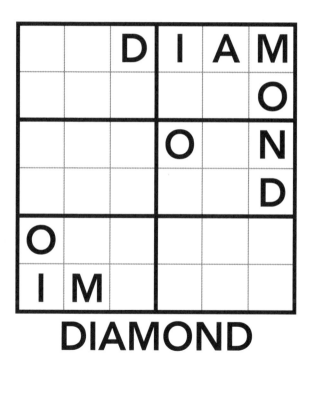

DIAMOND

Arrow Maze 4

Each move, jump from your current square to another square in the same row, column, or diagonal as permitted by the arrow or arrows provided. There are no dead ends here. Can you get from Start to Finish in 10 steps?

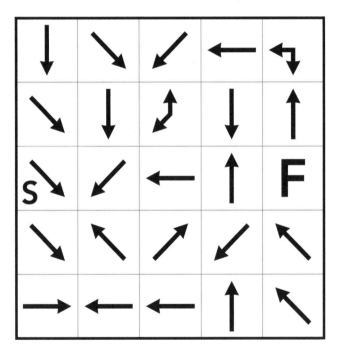

Tetra Grid 7

Drop each of the shapes into the grid in the order provided to spell ten six-letter words. Clues for the words have been provided next to the grid.

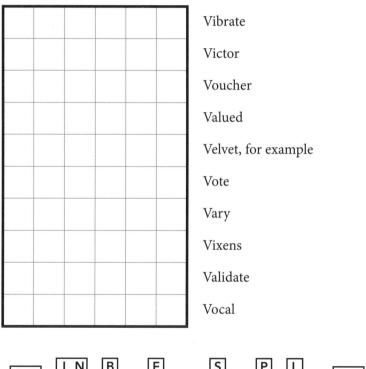

Vibrate

Victor

Voucher

Valued

Velvet, for example

Vote

Vary

Vixens

Validate

Vocal

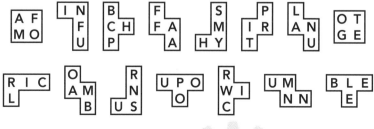

Big Sandwich 7–8

Stuff the space between the slices of bread, one letter per polygon, so that two words read down each column and two words read across the filling of the sandwich. The filling will form a phrase or compound word.

RI	C	BA	TAP	G
EN	VE	D	S	AM

Across Clue: Renewable

STA	CO	L	WI
E	K	P	E

Across Clue: Vacation

Numcross 7

Use the provided clues to fill the grid with numbers. No entry may start with a 0.

A	B	C		D	E
F				G	
		H	I		
J	K				
L			M	N	O
P			Q		

Across

A. J down + L across

D. I down converted from binary to base 10

F. D down + G across + O down

G. 2 × N down

H. D across × E down

J. K down × 10

L. O down + 5

M. 3 × P across

P. O down - 2

Q. A perfect square

Down

A. D across + O down

B. A multiple of D across

C. A palindrome

D. D across squared

E. Q across + 1

I. H across - Q across

J. F across × 3

K. Its digits sum to 18

N. Square root of Q across

O. 2 × G across

Word Sudoku 6

In the sudoku grid, enter one of each of six unique letters into each row, column, and rectangle without repetition.

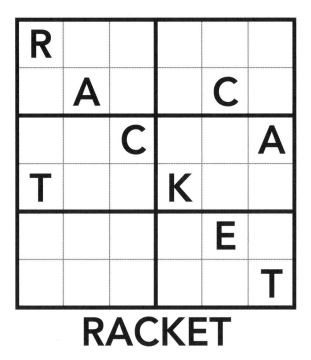

RACKET

Maze 4

Find your way from the top to the bottom.

Symbol Sums 8

The sums of five combinations of symbols have been provided. What is the value of each individual symbol?

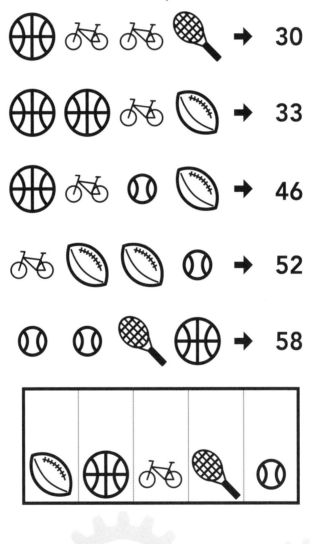

Triangulate 26–30

Use one letter from each triangle, in order from
left to right, to make three related words. Each
letter will be used once.

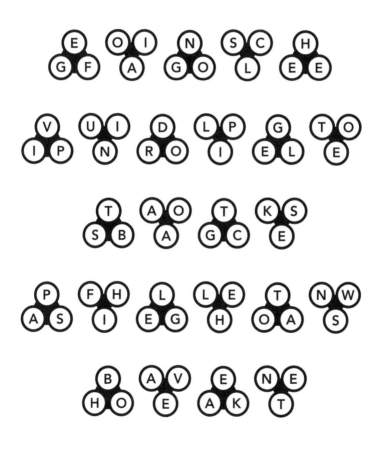

Tetra Grid 8

Drop each of the shapes into the grid in the order provided to spell ten six-letter words. Clues for the words have been provided next to the grid.

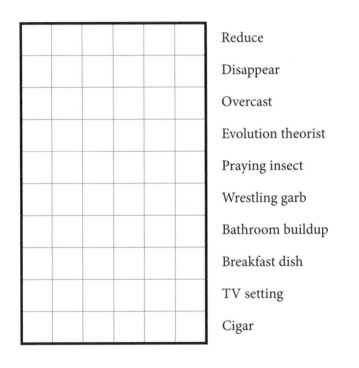

Reduce

Disappear

Overcast

Evolution theorist

Praying insect

Wrestling garb

Bathroom buildup

Breakfast dish

TV setting

Cigar

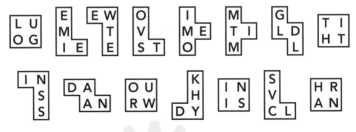

Big Sandwich 9–10

Stuff the space between the slices of bread, one letter per polygon, so that two words read down each column and two words read across the filling of the sandwich. The filling will form a phrase or compound word.

GA	B	FIL	HU
E	IT	S	S

Across Clue: Tropical

TI	TO	S	WA
ED	L	AP	E

Across Clue: Color-Changing

Story Logic 6

West Texas is famous for its Czech bakeries. One bakery is changing up its schedule for the next few weeks. Use the clues to match up the style of sausage roll being made with the employee responsible and how many dozen are needed.

		Dozens					Sausage Roll				
		10 Dozen	12 Dozen	16 Dozen	20 Dozen	24 Dozen	Breakfast Sausage	Cream Cheese	Jalapeño	Original	Pepperoni
Employee	Renee										
	Sakda										
	Toshihiko										
	Ursula										
	Vince										
Sausage Roll	Breakfast Sausage										
	Cream Cheese										
	Jalapeño										
	Original										
	Pepperoni										

There need to be 8 dozen more breakfast sausage rolls than the type of rolls Sakda will make.

Ursula is going to make the cream cheese sausage rolls.

There need to be more of the pepperoni sausage rolls than original sausage rolls.

There need to be 8 dozen more jalapeño sausage rolls than the type of rolls Renee will make.

Vince is meant to make more of his rolls than the number of breakfast sausage rolls being made.

Numcross 8

Use the provided clues to fill the grid with numbers. No entry may start with a 0.

Across

A. V down + 1
D. A perfect cube
F. U across + MM down
I. A across + MM down
J. E down + 10
K. 9 × MM down
L. D across + H down
N. KK across × MM down
O. Its digits sum to 18
Q. R across × 3
R. KK across + 20
S. KK down × 10
U. 8 × Q down
X. Consecutive digits in
   ascending order
Z. HH down × 2
BB. Square root of II across
CC. A palindrome
EE. N across, scrambled
GG. 3 × C down
II. A perfect square
JJ. Another palindrome
KK. KK down - 3
LL. QQ across + E down
OO. 5 × KK down
PP. Another perfect cube
QQ. Q down + 4

Down

A. D across - 5
B. One-half KK down
C. 4 × D down
D. JJ across + N down
E. D across in reverse
F. Y down - A down
G. Z across - 5
H. Another perfect square
M. A across + 2
N. The square root of
   AA down
O. Consecutive digits in
   ascending order
P. 3 × LL across
Q. QQ across - 4
T. Another palindrome
V. 3 × MM down
W. HH down - 5
Y. Contains one of each
   even digit: 0, 2, 4, 6, 8
AA. Another perfect square
DD. BB across - 2
FF. P down × 3
GG. QQ across × 3
HH. 2 × II down
II. Consecutive digits in
   ascending order
KK. Another perfect square
MM. DD down × 5
NN. MM down + D across

Arrow Maze 5

Each move, jump from your current square to another square in the same row, column, or diagonal as permitted by the arrow or arrows provided. There are no dead ends here. Can you get from Start to Finish in 9 steps?

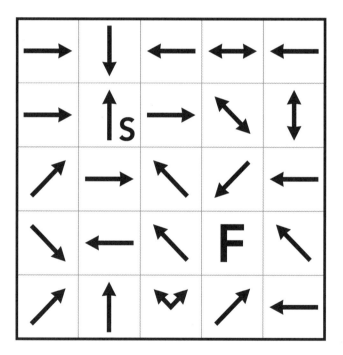

PE Class 2

Use the clues provided to find five answers
starting with the letters PE.

P E _ _ _ _   Small rock

P E _ _   Banana wrapper

P E _ _ _   King of the Hill matriarch

P E _ _   South American country

P E _ _ _   Two-finger hand sign

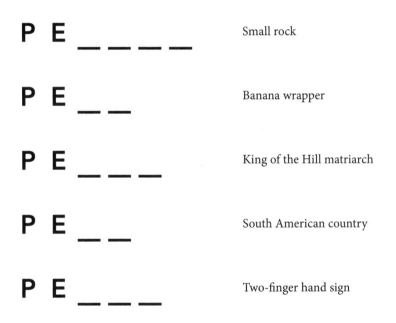

Cube Logic 6

Which of the four foldable patterns can be folded
to make the cube displayed?

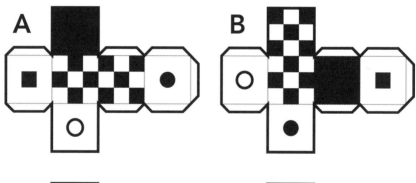

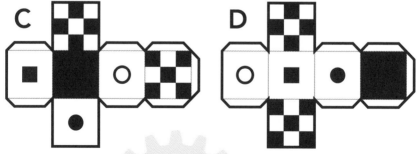

Rearrangement 9–10

Rearrange the letters in the phrase "SLACKED CHAIN" to spell a sandwich filling that keeps you coming back for more.

Rearrange the letters in the phrase "STRICT DOORMAN" to spell the kind of weather in which a good doorman wouldn't let you outside.

Symbol Sums 9

The sums of five combinations of symbols have been provided. What is the value of each individual symbol?

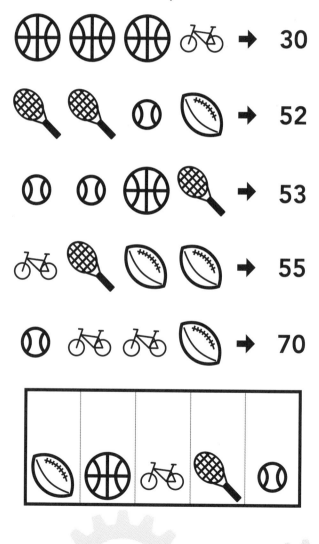

Tetra Grid 9

Drop each of the shapes into the grid in the order provided to spell ten six-letter words. Clues for the words have been provided next to the grid.

Voice box location

Dash

Type of store

Cheesesteak city

Almost the weekend

Rodent

Ruined grape

Belt fastener

Woolly animal

Snuggle

Shapes:

C A / L E

P A / D D

B / S / K L

A L / C U

R / R / B U

B / A I / C

P / F R / A

I L / I D

T / I N / E

Y / A Y / I

I / L E / L

P / U T / H

T / N T / T

T H / S O

R O A / R

Rearrangement 11–12

Rearrange the letters in the phrase "TRUE CAMPFIRE" to spell somewhere you'd put a photo from your camping trip.

Rearrange the letters in the phrase "HARDY WANDERERS" to spell some appliances that nomadic folk don't typically lug around.

Maze 5

Find your way from the top to the bottom.

PE Class 3

Use the clues provided to find five answers that
end with the letters PE.

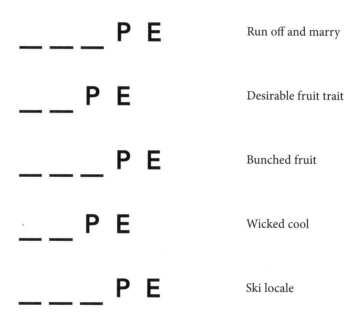

_ _ _ **P E**   Run off and marry

_ _ **P E**   Desirable fruit trait

_ _ _ **P E**   Bunched fruit

_ _ **P E**   Wicked cool

_ _ _ **P E**   Ski locale

Arrow Maze 6

Each move, jump from your current square to another square in the same row, column, or diagonal as permitted by the arrow or arrows provided. There are no dead ends here. Can you get from Start to Finish in 9 steps?

Hashtags 6

Use the hashtag clues provided to fill the grid with eight words. Four words with three letters should span the white squares in each row and column, skipping shaded squares. Four words with five letters use the full rows and columns.

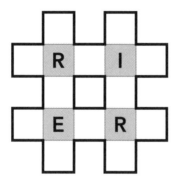

Threes

#24Hours #Literally

#Buddy

#Lady

#NapTime

Fives

#Chalice

#Journal

#Reproduce

#Stone #Oyster

Maze 6

In this maze, you may cross under paths using tunnels where indicated by arrows.

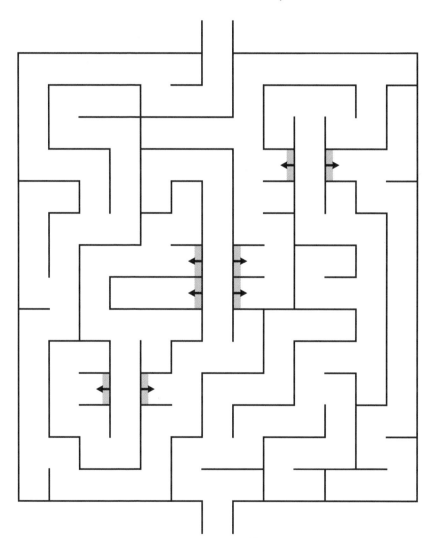

Answer Keys

Arrow Maze 1

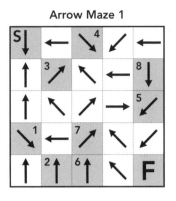

Arrow Maze 2

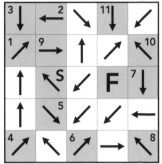

Arrow Maze 3

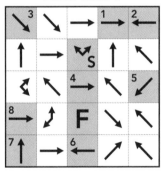

Arrow Maze 4

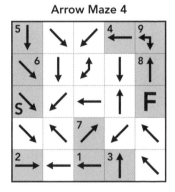

Arrow Maze 5

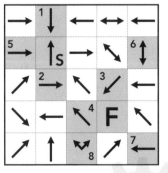

Arrow Maze 6

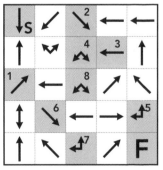

Big Sandwich 1

RI	LE	BE	S	MA
S	W	E	A	T
P	A	N	T	S
E	D	T	INT	H

Big Sandwich 2

RO	ME	BO	WA	BEL
B	A	S	I	L
P	L	A	N	T
E	T	S	T	S

Big Sandwich 3

LI	SE	S	S
S	N	O	W
F	A	L	L
T	T	AP	ING

Big Sandwich 4

OR	CH	S	S	L	T
B	U	T	T	E	R
C	O	O	K	I	E
S	MP	AR	ATE	E	AM

Big Sandwich 5

RA	C	GI	LI
G	O	L	F
C	A	R	T
E	RD	LS	TER

Big Sandwich 6

TE	B	DU	PE
R	E	S	T
A	R	E	A
M	AD	T	S

Big Sandwich 7

RI	C	BA	TAP	G
S	O	L	A	R
P	A	N	E	L
EN	VE	D	S	AM

Big Sandwich 8

STA	CO	GL	WI
R	O	A	D
T	R	I	P
E	K	P	E

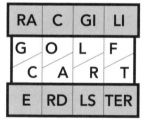

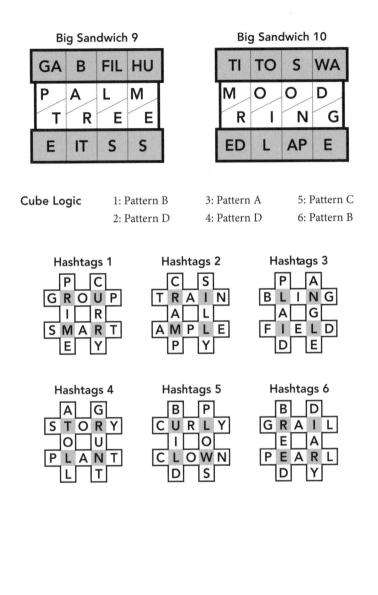

Big Sandwich 9

GA	B	FIL	HU
P	A	L	M
T	R	E	E
E	IT	S	S

Big Sandwich 10

TI	TO	S	WA
M	O	O	D
R	I	N	G
ED	L	AP	E

Cube Logic

1: Pattern B	3: Pattern A	5: Pattern C
2: Pattern D	4: Pattern D	6: Pattern B

Hashtags 1

```
  P     C
G R O U P
  I     R
S M A R T
  E     Y
```

Hashtags 2

```
  C     S
T R A I N
  A     L
A M P L E
  P     Y
```

Hashtags 3

```
  P     A
B L I N G
  A     G
F I E L D
  D     E
```

Hashtags 4

```
  A     G
S T O R Y
  O     U
P L A N T
  L     T
```

Hashtags 5

```
  B     P
C U R L Y
  I     O
C L O W N
  D     S
```

Hashtags 6

```
  B     D
G R A I L
  E     A
P E A R L
  D     Y
```

Maze 1

Maze 2

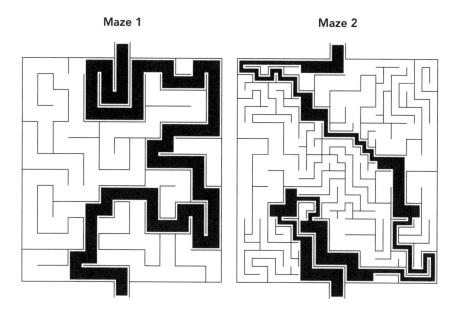

Maze 3

Maze 4

Maze 5

Maze 6

Numcross 1

2	3	1	■	1	1
1	0	2	■	4	2
■	■	3	1	4	1
1	5	4	1	■	■
8	4	■	4	5	6
1	3	■	1	2	0

Numcross 2

8	1	■	1	2	5
1	4	■	3	5	0
1	0	4	9	■	■
■	■	6	9	9	5
1	6	9	■	3	6
3	4	5	■	9	7

Numcross 3

■	■	3	2	1
■	6	6	6	6
5	4	■	7	0	1
1	0	8	■	2	7
■	8	0	1	0
■	2	1	6

Numcross 4

2	6	5	■	4	9
1	0	6	■	2	5
■	■	7	5	1	4
1	6	8	4	■	■
2	4	■	3	2	4
1	8	■	2	0	0

Numcross 5

2	9	■	1	3
3	1	■	3	6	6
4	6	9	5	■	■
■	■	3	6	9	7
1	6	9	■	9	3
2	4	■	8	1

Numcross 6

■	■	1	1
■	8	2	0	4	6
3	6	1	■	8	0
4	2	■	3	4	5
8	6	2	6	0	■
■	5	0

Numcross 7

5	8	8	■	1	1
1	8	1	■	2	0
■	■	1	1	1	1
5	5	8	0	■	■
4	5	■	1	1	4
3	8	■	1	0	0

Numcross 8

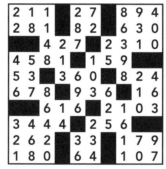

2	1	1	■	2	7	■	8	9	4
2	8	1	■	8	2	■	6	3	0
■	4	2	7	■	2	3	1	0
4	5	8	1	■	1	5	9	■
5	3	■	3	6	0	■	8	2	4
6	7	8	■	9	3	6	■	1	6
■	6	1	6	■	2	1	0	3
3	4	4	4	■	2	5	6	■
2	6	2	■	3	3	■	1	7	9
1	8	0	■	6	4	■	1	0	7

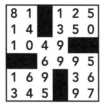

PE Class

1: Pesto, Perch, Penny, Peach, Pending
2: Pebble, Peel, Peggy, Peru, Peace
3: Elope, Ripe, Grape, Dope, Slope

Rearrangement

1: Bread Machine
2: Grid Notebooks
3: Waffle Cones
4: License Plate
5: Wooden Fence
6: Apple Orchard
7: Caramel Corn
8: Flea Market
9: Chicken Salad
10: Tornadic Storm
11: Picture Frame
12: Washer and Dryer

Story Logic 1   Kirsten, the sci-fi enthusiast in room 814, lost her pocketwatch.
Leigh, the anime lover in room 811, lost his utility belt.
Molly, the vlogger in room 815, lost her lanyard.
Nupur, the card gamer in room 813, lost her plastic sword.
Oliver, the role player in room 812, lost his cowboy hat.

Story Logic 2   January: Quincy Blvd., originally 11' 8", $1.1 million
April: Seventh Ave., originally 12' 1", $1.6 million
July: Roosevelt Dr., originally 10' 5", $2.6 million
October: Parker St., originally 11' 10", $2.1 million

Story Logic 3   Monday got 4.5 stars: Stir-Fried Squash from Midas Dairy & Co.
Tuesday got 3.5 stars: Fresh Tomato Pasta from Kale River Farms
Wednesday got 5 stars: Pepper Steak from Johnson Farms
Thursday got 2 stars: Eggplant Tart from Lincoln Ranch

Story Logic 4   First at 7:30 AM is Eduardo who gets a dirty chai.
Next at 8:30 AM is Becky who gets a green tea.
Next at 10:45 AM is Fabian who gets an espresso con panna.
Next at 11:45 AM is Dante who gets a white mocha.
Last at 12:45 PM is Chandra who gets a maple latte.

Story Logic 5   Sales is interviewing Harold at 9:30 AM.
Human Resources is interviewing Donna at 10:30 AM.
IT/Development is interviewing Esther at 11:30 AM.
Research is interviewing Filipe at 2:30 PM.
Marketing is interviewing Gozde at 3:30 PM.

Story Logic 6   Renee needs to make 16 dozen pepperoni sausage rolls.
Sakda needs to make 12 dozen original sausage rolls.
Toshihiko needs to make 20 breakfast sausage rolls.
Ursula needs to make 10 dozen cream cheese sausage rolls.
Vince needs to make 24 dozen jalapeño sausage rolls.

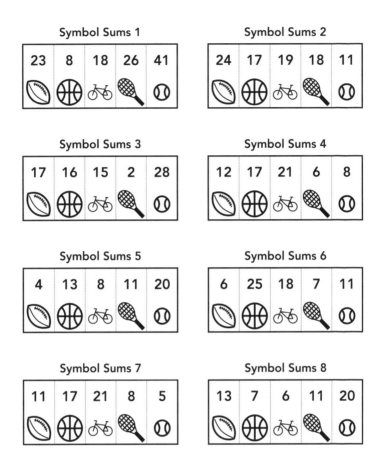

Symbol Sums 1

| 23 | 8 | 18 | 26 | 41 |

Symbol Sums 2

| 24 | 17 | 19 | 18 | 11 |

Symbol Sums 3

| 17 | 16 | 15 | 2 | 28 |

Symbol Sums 4

| 12 | 17 | 21 | 6 | 8 |

Symbol Sums 5

| 4 | 13 | 8 | 11 | 20 |

Symbol Sums 6

| 6 | 25 | 18 | 7 | 11 |

Symbol Sums 7

| 11 | 17 | 21 | 8 | 5 |

Symbol Sums 8

| 13 | 7 | 6 | 11 | 20 |

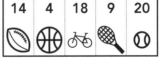

Symbol Sums 9

| 14 | 4 | 18 | 9 | 20 |

Tetra Grid 1

```
E L E V E N
G E N D E R
P R I N C E
R E D A C T
B A R T E R
W A S H E R
A C T I V E
S T E N C H
P A T R O L
D O O M E D
```

Tetra Grid 2

```
F A C I A L
C H U N K Y
W I N D O W
H A R B O R
S U R V E Y
L O T I O N
S P O N G E
T A T T O O
R E P O R T
D R I V E R
```

Tetra Grid 3

```
W O O D E N
C R E A M Y
R E S C U E
I S L A N D
S C R A P E
G R A T E D
R E P L A Y
P O T A T O
I N J U R Y
C R A F T Y
```

Tetra Grid 4

```
S P L A S H
R A V I N E
T O M A T O
D E B R I S
W A S A B I
E N E R G Y
A U T U M N
C E N T E R
S U R F E R
F I L T H Y
```

Tetra Grid 5

```
K I M C H I
C H E R R Y
Y E L L O W
T E S T E R
P A C K E D
E U R O P E
B R O N Z E
W H I S K Y
P E P P E R
M I N U T E
```

Tetra Grid 6

```
M E T R I C
D I A P E R
A F R I C A
S A L M O N
S C R E A M
R E C O R D
W I T H E R
T H R E A D
D E F E A T
S U N D A E
```

Tetra Grid 7

```
R U M B L E
W I N N E R
C O U P O N
F A M O U S
F A B R I C
B A L L O T
C H A N G E
P I N U P S
A F F I R M
M O U T H Y
```

Tetra Grid 8

```
S H R I N K
V A N I S H
C L O U D Y
D A R W I N
M A N T I S
T I G H T S
M I L D E W
O M E L E T
V O L U M E
S T O G I E
```

Tetra Grid 9

```
T H R O A T
S P R I N T
O U T L E T
P H I L L Y
F R I D A Y
R A B B I T
R A I S I N
B U B B L E
A L P A C A
C U D D L E
```

Triangulate

1:	Sugar, Honey, Syrup	16:	Drums, Flute, Viola
2:	Oyster, Shrimp, Salmon	17:	Yogurt, Cereal, Waffle
3:	Elk, Pig, Owl	18:	Joker, Heart, Spade
4:	Italy, Chile, Japan	19:	Earth, Pluto, Venus
5:	Naan, Pita, Roll	20:	Necklace, Earrings, Bracelet
6:	Black, Brown, Polar	21:	Bride, Groom, Rings
7:	Mosaic, Chrome, Safari	22:	Carrot, Potato, Radish
8:	Stool, Chair, Table	23:	Taste, Touch, Smell
9:	Beach, Cliff, Jetty	24:	Epoxy, Paste, Resin
10:	Save, Load, Quit	25:	Circle, Oblong, Square
11:	Tweet, Chirp, Growl	26:	Goose, Finch, Eagle
12:	Brunch, Supper, Dinner	27:	Purple, Violet, Indigo
13:	Board, Wheel, Grind	28:	Tote, Sack, Bags
14:	Decaf, Cream, Sugar	29:	Sheets, Pillow, Afghan
15:	Myth, Epic, Tale	30:	Bake, Oven, Heat

Word Sudoku 1

I	N	R	U	S	K
S	U	K	N	I	R
U	K	S	R	N	I
N	R	I	K	U	S
K	S	U	I	R	N
R	I	N	S	K	U

Word Sudoku 2

L	H	E	P	F	I
P	F	I	E	L	H
H	I	P	L	E	F
E	L	F	H	I	P
I	P	L	F	H	E
F	E	H	I	P	L

Word Sudoku 3

R	S	I	U	F	N
N	F	U	S	R	I
U	N	S	R	I	F
I	R	F	N	U	S
F	U	N	I	S	R
S	I	R	F	N	U

Word Sudoku 4

U	K	A	O	R	P
O	P	R	A	U	K
P	R	O	K	A	U
A	U	K	P	O	R
R	A	P	U	K	O
K	O	U	R	P	A

Word Sudoku 5

N	O	D	I	A	M
A	I	M	N	D	O
D	A	I	O	M	N
M	N	O	A	I	D
O	D	A	M	N	I
I	M	N	D	O	A

Word Sudoku 6

R	C	T	A	K	E
E	A	K	T	C	R
K	R	C	E	T	A
T	E	A	K	R	C
A	T	R	C	E	K
C	K	E	R	A	T

Thanks for solving!

Exercise Your Mind at American Mensa

At American Mensa, we love puzzles. In fact, we have events—large and small—centered around games and puzzles.

Of course, at 55,000 members and growing, we're much more than that, with members aged 2 to 102 and from all walks of life. Our one shared trait might be one you share, too: high intelligence, measured in the top 2 percent of the general public in a standardized test.

Get-togethers with other Mensans—from small pizza nights up to larger events like our annual Mind Games—are always stimulating and fun. Roughly 130 Special Interest Groups (we call them SIGs) offer the best of the real and virtual worlds. Highlighting the Mensa newsstand is our award-winning magazine, *Mensa Bulletin*, which stimulates the curious mind with unique features that add perspective to our fast-paced world.

And then there are the practical benefits of membership, such as exclusive offers through our partners and member discounts on magazine subscriptions, online shopping, and financial services.

Find out how to qualify or take our practice test at americanmensa.org/join.